The Weight Cut Bible

by Jon Fitch

Copyright © 2019 Jon Fitch

ISBN: 9798631482203

Cover Artist | Lily Mendoza
Editor | Robert Fisher

DEDICATION

To Coach Mo.

CONTENTS

Round 1 | Introduction....1

Round 2 | Meal Plans......2

Round 3 | Weight Cut.....9

Round 4 | Post-Weigh-In Meals...15

Round 5 | Fight Day....17

Victory | Conclusion...19

ROUND 1 | INTRODUCTION

If you're a fighter in MMA or another weight-class sport, you've probably wondered how you can effectively manage your diet and workout routines to consistently meet your weight class. I wondered the same thing when I first started as an MMA fighter 17 years ago, and I tried several different approaches before landing on my current one. Most of those approaches were frustrating and ineffective, and none of them could hold a candle to the strategy I'm about to tell you.

If you want to succeed in this sport, you need to put in the effort. That's as important for your diet as it is for your training. If you're flying by the seat of your pants and trying to cut all the weight just before weigh-in, you can't expect the best results, either for your health or your performance. You need to make a plan and follow through with it, and I'm here to show you my personal strategy for doing just that. It won't be easy, but in the end, it will save you time and effort and give you an edge for your next fight.

Don't underestimate the value of being able to consistently control your weight. Once you can do that, you'll spend less time worrying about making weight and more time doing what you enjoy. I will show you how to maintain a consistent baseline weight that can be easily adjusted in preparation for fight week, and how to tackle the dreaded weight cut successfully.

With this strategy in my toolkit, I meet my weight goals every time, and so can you.

ROUND 2 | MEAL PLANS

The meal plan is the first and most important part of my weight cut strategy. It is the bedrock that much of my success relies on. I didn't start using a meal plan until 2016, and once I did, I realized it was the last piece to my weight management puzzle. Switching to these pre-planned and scheduled meals made my weight cuts extremely predictable, and I had to rely less on the actual weight cut during fight week. That means less time spent sweating the weight off, an easier recovery, and a more successful experience overall.

I have to commit at least 4 weeks to the meal plan before I even start reducing my carb or protein intake. That's at least 6 weeks from the start of this plan to weigh-in. The meal plan is not for weaklings. If you can't control your eating, don't bother trying to follow these steps. You won't be nearly as successful with the rest of this strategy if you have poor eating habits. Without a good meal plan, you will have to cut more water the week of the fight, and you will be less likely to fully recover—which could lead to a fight where you get beaten up.

My meal plan is broken down into six meals, including two meals in the form of a protein shake. The goal is to split the meals up as evenly as possible throughout the day so that I eat every two or three hours. Eating on a regular schedule makes sure I put the nutrients into my body that it needs. The tight schedule also helps to keep me from snacking or breaking my diet. By the time I start getting hungry, it's time for another prepared meal. Having these meals prepped allows me to easily bring them with me, even if something pops up in my schedule. It is easiest for me to think of the food as fuel to the machine. I power through and eat the meals fast. I'll be able to enjoy my food on the weekend when I get a cheat meal or two—or when I taste sweet victory.

Because of my size and energy expenditure, I eat large portions of meat and eggs. I spend most of my training camp from 195–200 pounds, then I weigh in at 170 pounds a day before I fight. I eat the portions I do to maintain that weight. As I get closer to the fight, I can adjust my intake of food and lean out even more.

I will eat these amounts for about 4 to 8 weeks of training camp before I make any adjustments. I won't even give myself a cheat meal until I've been perfect on my diet for at least 3 weeks. I want to develop a solid foundation before I cut out any carbs or protein. As long as I am feeling good and my weight is 195–200 pounds, I leave things alone until about 3 weeks out from the weigh-in. Then I will bring my weight down within striking distance for the cut.

When I am in training camp, everything becomes part of training, including eating, sleeping, and the digestive process. Each meal becomes a little workout. At first, the frequency and volume of the meals were too much. I had to get my body used to eating the portions. Eating the eggs for breakfast took 45 minutes at first, but now I can crush them in 10 or less. The body adjusts fairly quickly to the food intake.

I'm going to take you through my meal plan one meal at a time. I will tell you what I am eating, how much of it I'm eating, and why I'm eating it. Other people might need to adjust the plan for their own needs, but this is what has worked well for me. This meal plan is ideal for a 6–12 week period of time, but I stay very close to this plan all the time. It keeps me pretty lean year-round. The idea behind it is to be as lean as possible while keeping muscle mass. That means low carbs and lots of protein. This helps me win fights and stay jacked.

First Meal: Breakfast

I wake up every weekday morning at 5:30 am to start breakfast. After breakfast, it's time to lift. I will hurriedly cook my eggs and warm my bacon so I can devour it and start my savagery. Driving to the gym to lift took too much time away from my day, so I set up a home gym to use instead. You have to get your priorities straight. I finish with my lift early so I have plenty of time to rest before my next workout. That workout is either 11 am for Brazilian jiu-jitsu or noon for MMA training.

My breakfast meal is eggs and bacon, pretty basic. Most people would get bored of it. I don't care, taste and boredom are irrelevant. I have work to do. I'm on a mission. Eating the same thing every day is just a part of it. I mean, it's bacon and eggs, don't be a baby! I cook the eggs on low heat with a big dab of butter and a scoop of cream cheese, 1 tablespoon each. I place the precooked bacon on top of the eggs to warm it up. I don't break the yolks until the white of the eggs is already cooked, then I scramble everything together. I precook the bacon in my portable convection oven, the same oven

I use to cook my chicken and fish.

Like I said, I eat large portions, and for breakfast, it's 8 whole eggs. I don't mess with plain egg whites. I like my eggs with yellows, and I'm unaware of any good reason why I should avoid eating whole eggs. With the 8 eggs, I eat 2 pieces of bacon. No juice or calories from beverages, I just drink cold water. It's not fancy, but it works. I eat this every day for breakfast. Sometimes on the weekend, I'll get a cheat meal for breakfast or I will fast.

Sometimes even I get tired of eating the same thing. If this happens, I can replace one egg with an ounce of meat. To switch things up I'll have 4 eggs and 4 ounces of meat. Either fish, chicken, or beef. Steak and eggs or salmon and eggs are good options. I keep the bacon though, because I love bacon.

Eggs are one food I don't like to eat cold or reheated, which means I have to cook them fresh every morning. This is a time suck for me. If I prepped the eggs ahead of time, it would save me a load of effort in the morning. For right now I don't mind, but someday I may lose this soft attitude against cold eggs.

Second Meal: Protein Shake

I have my second meal around 9:30 am to 10 am. This is after the morning lift and a few hours after the first meal. I drink the protein shake now to get nutrients to my muscles after the lift and to get me ready for my hardest workout, which starts at 11 am or noon. I don't want to have too much food in my stomach when I go in for hard training. That puts the shake in the perfect place to relieve my hunger but not fill me up too much for my next training session.

This shake can be made with milk or water. If I'm running a little heavy, I'll use water instead of milk. When I do use milk, I only use about a cup to a cup and a half of vitamin D milk. Along with a heaping scoop of protein powder, I add two other ingredients to the milk or water. The first is a tablespoon of Maca powder, which I use because it helps with energy and is also supposed to be a natural testosterone booster. The second is a tablespoon of raw cinnamon powder. The cinnamon is supposed to help reduce inflammation, which is a major obstacle to all athletes. A little bit of cinnamon can go a long way.

You might be thinking this shake is a nice little treat in your morning, but it's not. At least, mine isn't. The protein powder I use has no sugar, no artificial sweetener, and no added flavors. It doesn't have any flavor—unless "gross" is a flavor. I don't need it to taste good, though. I'm not on vacation getting a foot rub, I just need it to provide nutrients to my body. I don't sit around sipping on it and enjoying it. I slam the shake like it was a warm whiskey and get on with my day.

Along with this shake, I do one more thing: I eat a daily spoonful of raw organic coconut oil. Coconut oil is a good fat that does a lot for the body. The main reason I eat it is for joint and brain health. The fact that it keeps my skin and hair luxurious is a bonus.

Third Meal: Lunch

Team training for MMA is at noon at the American Kickboxing Academy, and it is my longest and most intense workout of the day. That's why lunch is my biggest meal, and usually has the most carbs with it. I keep my carbs simple and usually use white rice. Sometimes I will get fancy and eat sweet potatoes or Japanese sweet potatoes.

My lunchtime portion of carbs ranges from half a cup to a full cup of the cooked rice or potato, depending on my energy levels and if my weight is in the right spot. I will cook a week's worth of carbs when I'm prepping meals. After a week, the carbs will probably go bad or at least not taste great. I like using white rice the most because potatoes tend to get a little mushy after a couple of days.

For veggies, I usually go with broccoli. It tastes fine and I can eat it raw, which saves me time when getting my food ready. I can also buy it in bulk and it will last a couple of weeks while raw. Once it's cooked, you only have a few days before it goes bad or gets mushy. I don't want to make food runs to the store more than once a week. On occasion, I'll make asparagus with meal prep and I'll have that as my veggie for a few days. I'll be sure to eat asparagus if I can during fight week—it is a natural diuretic that will help you urinate.

You can eat as much of the veggies as you want, really. I usually keep it to half a cup, but if I'm extra hungry I may eat more. You aren't going to hold on to a lot of extra weight because of broccoli.

For my protein, I choose salmon, chicken, or beef. Usually, I go with organic chicken breast or ground beef, and I switch mostly for taste—my weight rarely runs high enough for me to need fish. If I'm on a tight budget or want to change things up, I can replace an ounce of meat with a whole egg. If my weight is running high, I will eat white chicken or salmon. The beef, appropriately enough, makes me a little beefy. For seasoning, I use pink Himalayan salt. That's it. Nothing fancy. I don't want to put anything into my body that might make it retain water or add empty calories. During the beginning of training camp, I eat 8 ounces of protein. I will stick with 8 ounces as long as I stay in my target weight range of 195–200 pounds.

I rank my proteins from lean to beefy. If I need to be a little leaner, I will go with the leaner protein. If I need to beef up, I will eat the beefier protein. My ranking goes like this, starting with the leanest option:

1. Whitefish (usually tilapia, cod, and halibut)
2. Other fish (my go-to is salmon and tuna)
3. White poultry (chicken breast)
4. Dark poultry (chicken thighs)
5. Beef (usually ground beef and sometimes ribeye steak)

I will eat pretty much the same lunch every weekday during my fight camp. I don't mess with the portions until about 3 weeks out from the weigh-in, because I don't want to lose too much weight too fast. I like a little extra size on me when I'm in fight camp. Hard sparring, grappling, and wrestling can take a toll on the body, so a little extra padding can help keep me healthy.

Fourth Meal: First Dinner

I eat my fourth meal from 4 to 5 pm, depending on my schedule with the kids that day. For me, this meal is most often just protein. Sometimes to mix things up a little I will add a little cheese or even some avocado to it. I don't want this meal to be too heavy, because I still have one last workout to do, and it's usually cardio-based. A full stomach is no good for that. On days that I have to pick the kids up from school, I usually end up eating in the car as I drive to get them. I'll eat it cold most days, too. I'd rather have 2 minutes of extra nap time than warm chicken.

Fifth Meal: Second Dinner

This meal comes after all my training is done, which can be any time from 6:30 to 8:30 at night. My energy level and weight will determine how many carbs I eat. I will eat anywhere from no carbs at all to a half cup of cooked carbs. If my weight is low or my energy feels low, I will eat more carbs. My vegetable portion for this meal follows the same rules as lunch. I usually eat a half cup of vegetables, but can pretty much eat as much as I want. Vegetables don't make you fat. The protein portion for this meal is the same as the lunch and first dinner portion: 8 ounces of salmon, chicken, or beef. This meal is the last solid meal I will eat for the day.

Sixth Meal: Second Shake

My last meal of the day is a protein shake that I drink from 9:30 to 10 pm. I can use whole milk if my weight is in the right range. Otherwise, water works fine. This shake doesn't use Maca powder like the first shake does, just cinnamon and unflavored whey protein. I drink my shake, brush my teeth, and go to bed. No time to get hungry and start to snack. The scheduled day keeps me from needing a snack and keeps me from thinking about food.

Weight Adjustment

After being on the same meal plan for a while, I developed a solid base, meaning my body would be the same weight consistently. Now that camp is winding down, it's time to start getting my body ready to make weight. The next thing I need to do is get my weight down into what I like to call "striking distance." Striking distance is a weight where, if push comes to shove, I could still make weight.

I spend most of my training camp at 195–200 pounds, but that's too much water weight for me to lose. At least, it's too much for me to lose and still be able to perform worth a damn. I need to slowly work my weight down over the next 2 to 3 weeks leading into fight week. My objective is to get to 182–185 pounds a week before weigh-ins. That way I can start fight week around 182 pounds. At that point I'll feel great, I'll be healthy, and I'll only have to deal with 12 pounds. No big whoop.

To start taking some pounds off, I begin reducing my protein. I want to lose the weight slowly, so I'll remove one ounce of protein at a time. For breakfast, I will switch to one piece of bacon and 7 eggs. For lunch and my two dinners, I will only have 7 ounces of salmon, chicken, or beef. I leave the shakes alone for now.

At this time, I change my carb amount at lunch as well. I limit the carb to a half cup, max—no more living like a king eating a whole cup. If my weight is high I can skip this carb, the second dinner carb, or both.

There's no reason to lose the weight too fast. It does me no good to get my body used to being small. I want to blow back up to a larger size once the weigh-in is over, and I can't do that if my body forgets how to be big.

Fight Week

This is where all the discipline comes together and pays off. Not having to stress about weight during fight week is a blessing. If everything has gone correctly with my meal plan during camp, I will be around 182 pounds on Monday of fight week. Most MMA fights happen on Saturdays, so that's the schedule I'm using here.

I make more reductions as fight week starts. I keep the single piece of bacon but reduce my eggs to four. Butter and cream cheese stays the same. My meals get reduced to three. I skip my second meal completely, and no more shakes at this point. It's fight week, so I'm not training the same way. No more multi-workout days. The workouts I do during fight week are light and easy. A lot of the week's focus is on recovery.

Lunch can be any time from noon to 4 pm, depending on my travel plans and promotional schedule, and dinner can be any time from 6 to 10 pm. Still, no shakes. These meals are the same: no carbs, 4 ounces of protein, and vegetables. You can eat as many vegetables as you want with these two meals until Thursday night. That's when the water weight cut starts.

The point of the reductions this week isn't to lose even more weight. They're meant to burn up the rest of my fat and clean out my system, preparing me to sweat a lot. Since this week is a recovery week, I'm not burning through nutrients as fast. That means I don't drop much weight, even though I reduce the protein. I want to maintain my weight so that I weigh about 178–180 pounds when I start my weight cut workout on Thursday night.

ROUND 3 | WEIGHT CUT

This is the most dreaded part: the actual weight cut. This is the process of removing water from your body so you will weigh less on the scale. It's been a long tradition in weight-class sports. The idea is to be as big and strong as possible for your weight class. The basic idea is this: you sweat out water and weigh in at a lower weight, then you drink back the water before you compete. Genius, I know. Until we find a better alternative, at least I have a system that makes it fairly easy to do.

I don't start the weight cut until late Thursday night, around 9 or 10 pm. The idea here is that I don't want to be close to my weigh-in weight (170 + 1 pound for a non-title fight) for very long. I want to keep the time that my body is depleted of water as short as possible. Official weigh-ins start at 9 am. My goal is to drop 6 to 8 pounds before I eat dinner. That's right—I make sure to eat dinner. You have to put fuel in the machine if you want it to work for you.

The best case scenario is that I lose enough weight to be at 172 + 1 pound, roughly 2 pounds over my contracted weigh-in weight. I have been within a pound of this range since starting the meal plan. The clean diet I'm on makes it really easy for me to break and maintain a sweat because I'm not putting any chemicals into my body that make me retain water. That's the objective of this workout: to sweat. That's it. This isn't a cardio workout or a test of strength, and I'm not trying to learn new skills. It helps to have fun with it and keep things light. Joke around and don't be too serious—it makes the time pass faster.

The idea here is to keep moving just enough to keep the sweat coming, without doing too much that can overheat the body. If the body overheats, you can be in trouble. I can't cut weight effectively if I get dizzy and pass out, and I don't need to break my body down or even hurt myself by hitting mitts or grappling too hard.

The first thing I do for this workout is suit up in my weight cutting gear. Having weight cutting gear is essential if you want to sweat the most with the least amount of work. First thing's first: Albolene. That's right, Albolene the makeup remover. I didn't learn about this miracle cream until I started fighting. When you put a thin layer of this stuff on your skin, it opens up your pores and helps you sweat. We look for every advantage we can get.

Once I'm greased up like a pig with my Albolene, I put on my sauna suit, or "plastics." Sauna suits come in many different forms. Some are of higher quality than others. I've found over the years that it's better to put your money into a higher quality suit if you can find one. Nothing worse than trying to shed pounds and you rip your plastics. That rip can cause a draft that could slow or stop you from sweating.

Once I have my plastics on, I put on my shirts. I usually wear a long-sleeve thermal shirt with a long-sleeve t-shirt over the top of it. After the shirts, I put sweatpants on over the plastic bottoms. Then a sweatshirt, usually hoodless—the hood just gets in the way. Most importantly, I must now tuck my shirts and sweatshirt into my sweatpants. To keep them tucked in, I have to pull the sweatpants up a little higher than normal and tie them in place. This is an ancient strategy passed through generations of wrestlers, from lips to cauliflower ears.

Doing this keeps all the heat in, which makes the workout more efficient. I don't want to work hard here—I'm not trying to push and break my body down, I'm just trying to lose a little water weight. I put on socks and wrestling shoes, and I like to tape my sweatpants around the ankle too like I'm afraid some critters are going to crawl up my leg. The last pieces to go on are hand wraps and MMA gloves.

My goal for this workout is to move as much as I need to maintain a solid sweat. The clock is set for 5-minute rounds with a minute break. I will stick to the clock as close as I can, but if I need to stop to take a breath I will. I may also need to take more than a minute to recover and start the next round. There is nothing wrong with stopping for a while. Even if I take a whole round off, it's okay. The key is that I am sweating. It has to be dripping sweat though, not just a moist forehead. I like to think of it as a faucet—once it's on, it's on. It doesn't help to keep turning the handle. If I push too hard, I could overheat.

The workout starts with a 2-round warm-up. I've done shadowboxing for 2 rounds, and I've jumped rope for one round and shadowboxed for another. With all my gear on, those are plenty good as warm-up rounds. I'm usually sweating good by the end of this warm-up. It's a good omen when there is butt crack sweat before I even start hitting mitts. Ideally, I want to do 3 rounds of mitts and 3 rounds of grappling-based drills. Again, I'm not going hard, I just want to move enough to sweat. I still use impeccable technique, of course. If I need to take a short break at any time, I do, as long as I keep sweating.

The 3 rounds of mitts are light and my coach keeps me moving. One thing he stays on my case about is footwork, as he should. Footwork should be perfect no matter how tired you are. If you're not a turd, you shouldn't move around like one. After I finish the mitt rounds, it's time to grapple. By now I've sweat a good amount and I'm running a little hot, and I will almost definitely stop and take a break at some point during these rounds if I haven't been taking breaks already. The first grappling round is spent closing the distance and getting in on the hips. The next round I focus on top control. In the last round, I work on getting up from the bottom. This is all done at a slow and controlled pace.

Once I've survived the grappling portion of the weight cut, it's time to cool down a bit. I spend the next round shadowboxing again. This allows me to start cooling down, but lets me keep the sweat flowing—you need to keep that faucet turned on. At the end of this shadowboxing, it's been 9 rounds of work. The next step is to do the mummy wrap. I will lay down on the mat still wearing my gear, and my coaches will cover me with towels. This helps keep me warm and sweating for an extended time. I will lay under the towels up to 15 minutes, or until I feel like my sweat has significantly slowed or stopped.

I have done things this way for the last five fights, and everything went like clockwork. I consistently lost about 7 pounds each time. After I get back home or to the hotel and I'm showered and dried off, I'm usually around 172–173 pounds. That means I get to eat.

Dinner

I don't believe in starving myself to make weight. The body needs to eat. The machine needs fuel, and it needs to sleep. At least, mine does. And if I don't get some food in my belly, there's a good chance I won't sleep much that night. It's a funny thing—when your body thinks it's dying, it won't let you sleep, no matter how tired you are. It wants you to get up and survive.

I focus a lot on losing enough weight during the workout that I can eat and drink more with dinner. It helps keep me motivated when I'm hot and tired. I just think about how good everything tastes when you are that depleted. The key here is that I don't want to go to bed any more than 4 pounds over my contracted weight. I usually float 2 pounds overnight, and 2 pounds in the morning is an easy cut in the sauna. That means if I get my weight to 2 pounds over after the workout, I will be able to eat and drink 2 pounds of food for dinner.

Believe it or not, 2 pounds is a decent-sized meal if you do it right. The trick is to not lose control of your drinking. It's really easy to drink 2 pounds of fluid (32 ounces) when you are thirsty. I make sure to save the drink for last. If I fill up on fluid, I won't have any room left for the nutrients I need to put into my body. I will usually have some kind of protein drink with ice to cram more nutrients into the fluid. It won't be the regular gross-tasting shake either. When you are this close to weighing in, it's okay to have a shake that tastes good.

I will eat 4 ounces of protein for this meal, usually chicken, and look to eat around 6 ounces of vegetables. Being depleted means my stomach can be pretty small at this time, and that can keep me from eating all of the veggies. At this point, I'm not even all that hungry—I mostly want to drink water. But I make sure to eat my food so I have the nutrients in my body that I need. The machine can't run on empty.

I keep my fluid intake at around 8 ounces, which is half a pound right there. After I finish my food and drink, I'm probably around one and a half pounds heavier. That gives me some wiggle room. I could drink another 8 ounces of fluid, or I could give myself another treat. If I can, I'll freeze some grapes to eat. If I can't freeze them, I'll eat them plain. I will eat a few grapes, up to a full 8 ounces, or I might skip this completely and just go straight to sleep. It will all depend on how I feel that night.

The frozen grapes are a real treat for me. Freezing them makes me eat them more slowly, and the peels on the grapes help push everything through my digestive tract. This usually helps me go to the bathroom in the morning, which takes off a little extra weight. After dinner, I'm still depleted of water and very thirsty. Snacking on a few ounces of frozen grapes, or even unfrozen ones will take my mind off of drinking water until I'm ready to lay down and go to sleep.

Bedtime is usually around 1 or 2 am. My goal is to get around 4 hours of sleep before I have to get up and get in the sauna. This is easier said than done. Like I said before when your body thinks it's dying, it wants you to stay awake so you don't, and that's a lot worse if you don't eat enough. I've had nights with zero sleep before. Fortunately, since I started with the meal planning, I have been able to sleep like a baby for at least 4 hours while sucked out.

Sauna Time

In recent years the athletic commissions have changed the way weigh-ins are done. It used to be that you weighed in around 4 or 5 pm, which meant having to hold your weight for a lot longer than you do now. It's not a good idea to be depleted for that long. The longer you stay depleted, the harder it is on your body, and that can affect performance. Moving the weigh-ins to 9 am was a great move for everyone. Now you hold your weight for a shorter time, and you get more time to replenish and recover.

I get up at 6 am to cut the rest of the water weight in the sauna. If you rely on a traditional sauna, you could run into some issues. There might not be a sauna close to the hotel, and you could have to drive 30 minutes just to get to one. Even then, the sauna could suck, and you might end up sharing it with all the other fighters on the card. That can be annoying. To guarantee I don't have those problems, I bring my portable infrared sauna. They cost less than $200 and work great. That way I can sit in the sauna in my room and watch TV or read something to pass the time.

I also really like my portable infrared sauna because the infrared light penetrates the muscles deeper at a lower temperature. This means I can get a good sweat going without overheating. In my opinion, that makes it safer to use than a traditional sauna. The amount of time I spend in the sauna will depend on how much I weigh. On a couple of occasions, I didn't have to use the sauna at all—I floated 3 pounds overnight and was able to just lay down until weigh-in time.

I've found that when I use my sauna, it takes about 30 minutes to lose a pound. If I'm 2 pounds over, it's going to take me an hour to lose it. The key here is that I don't start the clock until I break a sweat. It usually takes about 15 minutes to get the juices flowing, but it has taken me as long as 30 minutes before. Once the sweat does start, it flows like a river. The clean diet stops my body from being stubborn and holding onto the water like it's money.

Since I know it takes about 30 minutes a pound, I know how long I have to sit in the sauna, and I don't keep getting out to check weight. I need to keep that sweat flowing until the weight is off. When you are already really depleted of water and you stop sweating, it can be difficult, if not impossible, to start sweating again. Luckily the portable sauna allows me to watch TV, look at my phone, read, or just talk to my coaches while I cut. This keeps me from thinking about how uncomfortable I am and makes things easier.

After I've been sweating for the estimated amount of time I need, I get out and check weight. If I'm still over, I go back to the sauna. Fortunately, this has never happened while using this system. When I get out of the sauna, I'm usually right on or under my contracted weight. If I happen to be under the contracted weight, I will drink some fluids to get it right on. There is no benefit from weighing less than you need too. Be on weight, not under.

Once my weight is good, I will head down and check-in with the commission for the weigh-in. I prefer to get on the scale as close to 9 am as I can. That way I have even more time to rehydrate and recharge with food. As soon as the official weigh-in and medicals are done, it's time to eat.

ROUND 4 | POST-WEIGH-IN MEALS

What I eat for my first meal after making weight might surprise you—it sure as hell surprised me when my meal coach Manny told me. He had me eat two 2x2 cheeseburgers from In-N-Out, washed down with half a small diet coke. No fries. He told me that once I made weight it was okay to add carbs to my meals, just not too many. I make sure to balance my carbs with my proteins.

Since your body hasn't had any carbs in the past week, when you do eat them your body soaks them up. The diet coke is supposed to have a chemical in it that helps your body absorb the nutrients better. It's an old bodybuilding trick to help your muscles look even more swollen. Looking extra jacked is just a byproduct of the nutrient absorption into the muscles, it's not the point of doing it—but I've got to admit, it's a pretty awesome byproduct.

I haven't always had access to In-N-Out while making weight, which means I have to find an alternative place to get my cheeseburgers. The key is to find a place that has quality ingredients, no fake meat or food that's too greasy. I eat this meal as soon as I can after I make weight. No need to dilly dally—the sooner I get it eaten, the sooner it will be digested enough for me to eat another meal.

I will lie down after I eat to rest and digest, and I'll continue to drink fluids on and off for the rest of the night. I mostly drink water but will mix in a little Gatorade, coconut water, Pedialyte, and some protein shake too. Drinking water alone isn't enough, because in addition to needing to rehydrate, I want to make sure I replenish the nutrients I've lost. One of the big signs I look for to gauge my recovery is how prone I am to cramping. At first, you cramp easily. By bedtime, the cramps should mostly be gone. The other way I gauge my hydration is the color of my urine. I need it to be crystal clear. If it's dark yellow and smells, you've got a lot more work to do.

My stomach will get bloated from the food and drink, but it's okay. It will

14

settle itself long before fight time. Usually, I'm feeling back to normal by noon the next day. I lie down and sip on fluids until it's time to leave for the mock weigh-ins, which are usually in the late afternoon. While I'm there, I'll bring my water and maybe some fruit to snack on. As soon as the mock weigh-ins are done, it's time to eat a big meal.

The first dinner for me is usually at a nice restaurant. This meal is slow and I'll have as many of my crew with me as I can. Usually, I go for a big juicy steak. I still keep my intake balanced between the protein and carbs, and I avoid greasy food and sugar. Finishing off a basket of bread without getting in your protein is a bad idea. I'll also have a smaller amount of veggies to help with digestion. I'll often order too much to eat in one sitting so I'll have food to take with me to eat later for my second dinner.

The second dinner isn't anything formal. It's almost always leftovers from the first dinner, although sometimes I will order food from somewhere else. I've been lucky enough to stay in hotels with decent food. I don't eat snack foods that are full of sugar, but I might have some fruit with it or drink a protein shake. My goal is to get my weight up as close to 190 pounds as I can before I go to sleep. The closest I've gotten so far is 189 pounds. When I finally go to sleep, I'm a little bloated and fully hydrated, because I've been sipping on fluids since I stepped off the scale. I make sure that my pee is clear and I'm no longer cramping before I sleep.

ROUND 5 | FIGHT DAY

On fight day I wake up early, around 6 am, so I can eat and get some nutrients and more water into my body. I do this because the closer the fight gets, the more my nerves kick in, and I lose my appetite. I did a lot of work to put the weight back on and I don't want it to melt away because I didn't eat on fight day. I keep breakfast simple and still try to balance the protein and carbs. Usually, I eat eggs and carb and sometimes I'll even do steak and eggs. My usual carbs are sourdough toast or potatoes. I don't normally finish this meal. I'll force-feed myself and eat what I can. When I can't eat anymore, I'll go back to sleep.

I spend most of fight day sleeping and resting, which keeps me from overthinking the fight and mentally wearing myself out. It also gives me a chance to fully recover from the weight cut. Making weight is the fight before the fight, and you must recover from it or you will pay dearly. Sometime in the afternoon, any time from 11 am to 3 pm, I'll eat lunch. Most of the time I eat leftovers from breakfast. I'll also have a protein shake and eat whatever protein bars I have left. This isn't a huge meal—by now my stomach is pretty small from the nerves. After I eat, I'll go back to resting and sleeping until it's time to report to the arena.

The last meal I eat before battle isn't a full meal. My place on the card will affect how much I try to make myself eat. If I'm on the undercard, I have to report earlier and have less time to eat. In that case, I sometimes don't eat at all. If I'm the main event, I will do my best to eat at least half of a chicken sandwich. Most athletic commissions don't allow food or outside beverages in the back dressing rooms, but they supply all the water you need. During fight day, I excrete a good amount of the food and water that I took into my body the day before. I want to be as heavy as possible for the fight. That's why it is important to continue to eat and drink the day of the fight. I can't let the nerves get to me or I won't fully recover from the cut, and I might be flat or

16

even gas during the fight. It's also important I don't overeat and end up bloated come fight time.

By fight time, all the eating is done. I have my body back and it feels good. I will feel better than I have at any point during the training camp. All the work is done, the weight was made, and I've fully recovered from camp and the cut. I will sip on water as needed up until it's time to make the walk to the cage. The cage door closes, and it's fight time.

VICTORY | CONCLUSION

If you've made it this far, congratulations—you now have the tools you need for a more successful weight cut strategy. Following the methods I've shown can make for a smoother experience on fight week, so you won't have to rely on extreme diet restrictions and sweating out before the weigh-in.

Like I said, my meal plan is not for weaklings, and by now you can tell I was serious when I said it is the bedrock of this whole strategy. For me, it's worth it. No uncertainty of will I or won't I make the weight, no worrying about scrambling at the last minute because I didn't make the progress I expected. This strategy gets me the results I need and leaves me worry-free so I can focus on other parts of my training. I hope it brings you the same success.

TESTIMONIAL

"Jon Fitch's method has made an incredible impact on both my career and also my lifestyle. All these people come out with diet plans and tell you what to do, but I was looking for something more than that. I wanted something to implement in my life moving forward and not just only for the two to three months of a fight camp.

As a professional MMA fighter, the food I put in my body is key. I need the right nutrients for my workouts and training. I have to make weight. I have to keep my weight low even when I'm not fighting. Not only that after I make weight I need to eat the right thing. Some people go off the deep end and eat anything and everything they want after making weight.

Jon Fitch's method breaks down what, when and why to eat specific foods throughout these processes. As one of my favorite fighters back in the day, he has a lot of knowledge and has the success to prove it. Now I have the success to prove it too. Ever since I turned to his method, I can feel the difference and I've been undefeated ever since."

-Ian Butler | Bellator Fighter

ABOUT THE AUTHOR

Jon Fitch is a seasoned Mixed Martial Artist who's been in the professional MMA world since the birth of the sport. With almost 20 years of experience and 42 professional fights under his belt, he is one of the best welterweights on earth.

When he's not in the cage, he hosts seminars, offers personal training and is a huge advocate for fighters rights and is a member of the Mixed Martial Arts Fighter Association that has been lobbying Congress to add MMA to the Ali Act and is fighting for future fighters rights in a class action antitrust suit filed against the UFC. In his offseason, you can find him looking for adventures with his two sons, playing the ukulele, writing and working on his podcasts. He currently fights for Bellator and resides in San Jose, CA.

Items used in this weight cutting system can be found online at
https://www.amazon.com/shop/jonfitchdotnet

@jonfitchsmash

http://jonfitch.net

BONUS CHAPTER
FAILING UPWARD | DEATH BY EGO | BOOK ONE

Jon Fitch takes you back to the early days of Mixed Martial Arts by sharing his old journal entries and reflecting on them. Follow along as he goes from a struggling Division 1 wrestler to MMA superstar. See firsthand what it was like back in the wild west early days of the sport. Before the sport was regulated and there were no guarantees that you would even get paid. See for yourself how the sport evolved, how AKA evolved and how Jon fitch the fighter and the man evolved. Available on Amazon!

CHAPTER 11 | BRAZILIAN JIU-JITSU AND GIRLS

Not having to focus on training for a fight allowed me to focus on Brazilian jiu-jitsu. Unfortunately, it also gave me time to be distracted by girls. When I was at Purdue there weren't that many girls around. At least not that many that were my type. Purdue is an engineering school. Way more guys than girls there. Being a wrestler also meant you disappeared for most of the year too. Not much time for girls. Girls that age usually want to be out partying or at least socializing on some level. Wrestlers are cave dwellers for 4 or 5 months out of the year. When we finally do come out of the cave, we're usually wearing sweatpants.

San Jose was different. Way different. There were girls everywhere. And they were beautiful. I did my best to stay away but did I mention they were everywhere. I did work at a bar and girls do go to gyms. I wasn't used to getting attention like this either. From what I could tell, west coast girls really liked Midwest boys. Or maybe it was just me?

Having fights to train for made it easier to keep myself focused. Fight camp helped me stay away from distractions. After my birthday however, I started to focus more on just one of the distractions — a younger girl I started calling "the student" in my journal. When we met, she was 18 and still in high school. I had no idea how old she was until the day I got her phone number. I was talking to some other girls at the time, but within a month she had me locked down.

I didn't mind because she never got in the way of training and all we ever did together was have fun. Plus, we both kind of knew that it was only going to be a summer thing since she would be leaving for school in the fall. So, there was no pressure.

I had started to make some major strides in my skill set. Everything was getting better. The down time in between fights sucked; it still does. It means less money and its way harder to stay motivated. Luckily, I forced myself to stick to my training routines regardless of whether or not I had a fight lined up.

I've seen a lot of guys get discouraged and stop coming in to train because of those very same reasons. I used the down time to make myself better. I let improving my skill set be my motivation. I was having a great time doing it too. I mean why not. I was surrounded by great people and there was always good training to be found.

2/25: Sparred with little Dave today. He said I am getting better. I sense some tension in the gym over big Mike's training. The guys going to big shows get special training. Lynn gets left out. That's crap. I must remember to make sure Lynn does my training in the future. Shoulders are sore. Pummeling with big Mike and the tournament last Saturday are having an effect. Just like the first couple of weeks of wrestling season in college and high school. Must remember to do my rotator cuff exercises.

2/26: Sparred again with little Dave today. I have improved greatly. In another year my standup will be money. Things are coming together. I got plane tickets back home today. Will be in Indiana from March 11 to the 22nd. It will be fun. Good time to be home. Looks like I won't fight till May anyways. I should be able to get some workouts in back home too. Do some wrestling with Purdue's team.

2/27: Sparred with Ebersole today. Southpaws are tricky. I did well with him though. I felt good. Been talking to dirty D. Don't know if anything will happen with that. It's hard to tell. The student is cool too. Trying to phase out the Puerto Rican girl. Taking training easy till I leave for home. Just stick to technique. Time for a nap.

2/28: No one came to class today. I helped Kelly Dullanty with his, kids, class though. Went on a hike this morning with people and dirty D. I think I will try and let my crush fade. Hopefully it will. Don't think she is interested anyway. If she makes a move, then cool. If I say something or do something, I could just make things weird for everyone. I'll just stick to being a big dog. Don't need to get all caught on a girl anyways. I came out here for a reason. Must not get sidetracked. Things are going well. If I keep this pace, the sky's the limit. I will be leaving for home soon. It will be nice to see old faces. I must remember that desire is the root of all suffering. Sacrifice is the key to greatness.

Close your eyes and see.

3/1: Sparred this morning with Trevor and Christian. Felt really good. I have come a long way. Have to keep my hands up. Those kicks come up fast. Still confused about that girl. Think I'll just forget about it. Too confusing. Need to rest now. 11:20 p.m.: Learned some cool armbars tonight. Having fun in class. Using technique, a lot. Feels good.

3/2: Workouts went well. Lynn wants me to work on a left front kick to counter my opponent's right low kick. Going home next Thursday. Can't wait. Been focusing on technique lately. Will start training 100% when I get back from my trip. Will spar tomorrow. Sparring is fun. I like it a lot. Having fun with it. I like the phrase "close your eyes and see." I want to use it for my shirts and things. I should get a copyright for it. I will tell AC about it. See if he can use it in some shirt design ideas. I got Ogre's number too. So, I can get him to do the shirts for me.

3/3: Sparred today with Trevor. Did well. I am out of shape, so I couldn't put the pressure on him I wanted. We were doing takedowns too, but I wasn't trying to take him down. I didn't fight his takedowns much either. Wanted to focus on my standup. Having a hard time still finishing subs. Getting into a lot of positions for subs, just not able to finish. My guard is getting good too. Giving people fits as they try to pass. Still confused with the dirty, dirty. Can't figure her out. Things are good with the young-in. Trying to phase out the Puerto Rican girl slowly.

3/5: Sparred with Trevor again today. When I check kicks, I have to be moving forward or at least have my weight coming forward. Otherwise I can get swept. I did well today. Standup is coming, so is my ground game. Bob wants me to try and get into the pro division at Grapplers Quest. Jake Shields is in it. So, I might be able to get in it. There is prize money for winning but I would have to cover all other expenses. Might do it, I don't know.

3/6 4:00 a.m.: Thinking about doing Grapplers Quest. I'm going to send an email to the owner. See if I can get into the super fight tourney. It's late, couldn't sleep. Too many Red Bulls. Scraped some bits of weed from my pocket in my jeans. That's so dirty. It went up fast. Then I had to smoke the resin. Now at least I think I will be able to sleep. Need to get a hold of AC about my new saying, "close your eyes and see." Need to call Tony and Shea, see if they need anything from the Midwest. I'm sure they don't. I am still confused. For the first time in my life, I'm getting a lot of attention from women. Don't know what it is. I can't seem to let myself get close to any of them though. Won't let myself care about them. JT seems to have been the final straw. Broke my back. Told her she would be the last. Looks like that might be true. I hope it's not, but I don't see it going any other way. Maybe someday, but I am so old now. 26, am I going to be too old to have kids by the time I care about anyone again. Sucks.

3/8: Sparred with Brian and a little with Clint. Felt very good. Kicks feel good. Keeping myself safe. Can't wait to go home Thursday. Need to make some calls, let everyone know when I'll be around. Didn't go to Bjj tonight. Hard to stay motivated when I am leaving soon. I am going to the beach tomorrow. Going with dirty D. Don't know if it will be just us or not. Going to watch a movie Wednesday night with the student. It's been a while. Watching at home.

3/9: Did not train today. Went to the beach. It was nice. Going to spar tomorrow, then that will be the last workout till I leave. I don't like having to leave Bricks for so long but it's the only way right now. Purdue did really well at BigTens. They finished 6th. Ben Wissel made it through.

Barefoot shoe maker.

3/10: Lynn held mitts for me today. Leaving for home tomorrow. Can't wait.

3/23: Got back from Indiana yesterday night. It was a good trip. Saw lots of people in Indy, Purdue and the Fort. Got pretty fucked up a couple of times. Worked out with Dav. Submitted him a few times. Never did that before. Worked out with a freshman at Purdue. He is going to be a heavyweight. He was okay. Jake O'Brian his name was. My parents missed me. I played a lot with my nephews, they're great. My brother and his wife are good, too. I think I really do like Cali. It feels like home almost. At least it feels as much like home feels like home now. It doesn't. Don't know anyone now but I do, it's weird. It will always be home I guess. I took another risk again with a girl. Sooo stupid. I am so dumb. I always do this and I always get crushed. Always. Got back to training. Starting light. Ease into full speed by Monday. I think I am fighting in the WEC in May. I have months to get ready. The guy is Jason Von Flue. Bob says be ready for leg locks.

Work is the curse on the drinking class.

This piece of time really set the foundation for the rest of my career. I could have let the break between fights allow me to become distracted or discouraged. I could have used it as an excuse to get a real job or used it as a reason not to train. It would have been easy too. Girls to play with, beautiful weather and the beach was only 25 minutes away. I could have fallen back into heavy drinking and partying like most people my age were doing.

Instead, I doubled down on training. I spent 4 to 8 hours a day at the gym. I also began to focus all my attention on one girl. I was calling her "the student" in the journal, at least at first. Once we became girlfriend and boyfriend I started referring to her as Cheeks.

The student snuck up on me. I was crushing on one girl and hanging out with another when I met her. She worked part-time at the gym. We started talking casually and hanging out before she started work. We would go on walks with Bricks and talk. I wasn't really trying to get a girlfriend, but I ended up with one. The difference in our age kept me from thinking that anything would come from us hanging out. Boy was I wrong.

During my trip home to Indiana, I started to notice life happening. People set off on their own journeys. Things change. People change. People move away. Your hometown isn't really your hometown anymore. It's just a place you used to live. Normal grown up stuff you go through and no one tells you about. And if they did, I probably wasn't listening. Young people are often hard of hearing. At least I was.

I remember going back and not having anyone to call to hang out with. Only one of my good friends from high school, Gabe, even lived in town. If he wasn't available to hang out, I didn't have anything to do. I've never been one of those guys that goes to the strip club by myself.

I hadn't had a fight to look forward to for what seemed like forever. Finally, something solid to prep for. At least solid for those days. A chance to fight on a WEC card in May. I was doing a great job of sticking to my training schedule and focusing on making small improvements every day. This kept me going, but there is nothing that lights a fire under you like a fight does.

Made in the USA
Columbia, SC
13 October 2020